children's
Certificates of
Accomplishment

The Hill Family

...rtifies that _____
...age Adventure 1 and has taken an important
...wards learning the _____

...age Grade: _____

To order additional copies of this book, contact:
Xlibris
1-888-795-4274
www.Xlibris.com
Orders@Xlibris.com

ISBN: Softcover   978-1-4363-7719-5

Print information available on the last page.

Rev. date: 02/22/2020

Preschool Diploma

Congratulations

Victor Hill

You have completed Preschool and are awarded
this Diploma in recognition of your accomplishments.

Proudly presented at _Keith Street Pre-School_
(School)

in _Cleveland, Tenn._   on _May 30, 1991_
(City)   (State)   (Date)

By _Beverly Wade_

T-335 ©1980 TREND enterprises, Inc., St. Paul, MN 55164

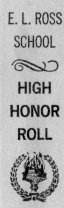

E. L. ROSS SCHOOL

DISTINGUISHED HONOR ROLL

E.L. Ross Elementary School

SECOND PLACE

FIELD DAY

E.L. Ross Elementary School

FIRST PLACE

FIELD DAY

E. L. ROSS SCHOOL

HIGH HONOR ROLL

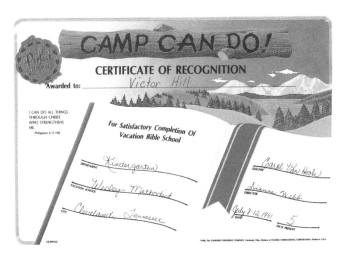

CAMP CAN DO!

CERTIFICATE OF RECOGNITION

Awarded to: _Victor Hill_

I CAN DO ALL THINGS THROUGH CHRIST WHO STRENGTHENS ME.
Philippians 4:13 NRB

For Satisfactory Completion Of
Vacation Bible School

DEPARTMENT _Kindergarten_

VACATION SCHOOL _Wesley Methodist_

CITY _Cleveland, Tennessee_

TEACHER _Carol Van Hook_

DIRECTOR _Dianne Webb_

DATE _July 8-12, 1991_

DAYS PRESENT _5_

©1998, the STANDARD PUBLISHING COMPANY, Cincinnati, Ohio, Division of STANDEX INTERNATIONAL CORPORATION. Printed in U.S.A.

Award
of
Participation

Thanks to

Victor Hill

for successfully completing

the Read Aloud Project.

READ a Book and have an ADVENTURE

Tennessee Reading Association

1

Certificate

Awarded To

Victor Hill

For Completion Of
Vacation Bible School
At The
North Cleveland
Church of God
June 10-14, 1991

Certificate of Achievement

SHERIFF DANIEL R. GILLEY'S CERTIFICATE OF

ACADEMIC EXCELLENCE

Awarded To   VICTOR HILL

on this day   MAY 26, 1995

In Appreciation Of Good Citizenship In Bradley County

SHERIFF DANIEL R. GILLEY

Music Award

Victor Hill

has participated with distinction in the

Cleveland City Schools
Elementary Chorus

In recognition of your contributions

this award is presented

this 30th day of May 1997.

signed Dale Harmeson

Cleveland City Schools

2000
Spelling
Bee

Presented To:

Victor Hill

FOR OUTSTANDING PERFORMANCE IN SPELLING

Given this 7th day of March, 2000

Nancy Boardman   Frederick D. Denning
SPELLING BEE COORDINATOR   DIRECTOR OF SCHOOLS

CERTIFICATE
OF
Attendance
Cleveland City Schools

THIS CERTIFIES THAT

Jamie Hill

HAS BEEN IN ATTENDANCE EVERY DAY FOR THE SCHOOL YEAR

1997-1998

Marion Kerr
Teacher

Ann B. Culbreth
Principal

Certificate of Participation

This Certifies That

Victor Hill

Merits grateful recognition as a participant in

A Spelling Contest

And is hereby awarded this certificate By

Tau Eta Omega Chapter
Alpha Kappa Alpha Sorority, Inc.
Organization

Cleveland, Tennessee
City and State

on this *8th* day of *June* 19 *96*

Cynthia Holmes   *Linda J. Wilson*

Brownie Troop 132

Presented to

Jamie Hill

Investiture and Rededication Ceremony
October 30, 1997

Carolyn R. Schween
Carolyn R. Schween, leader

Certificate of Achievement

at

Lee University Basketball Camp

Victor Hill

Date _June 27_ 19 _97_

Cleveland, Tennessee

Larry Carpenter
Camp Director

Home of the Flames

ROPE FOR HEART

06-3904 (DEV)

♥ American Heart Association

For outstanding service in advancing cardiovascular health and fitness and generating public support for the fight against heart and blood vessel diseases.

CERTIFICATE OF
APPRECIATION
PRESENTED TO:

Victor Maurice Hill

E. L. ROSS SCHOOL

Sponsored by the

American Alliance for health physical education recreation and dance

---

NATIONAL PHYSICAL FITNESS AWARD

presented to

Victor Hill

for commitment to
and achievement in physical fitness
for improved health and performance.

Bill Clinton
President of the United States

A Program of the President's Council on Physical Fitness and Sports

---

Certificate of Achievement

Victor Hill
Student Name

of

Cleveland Middle School
School Name

has successfully completed

PERSONAL ECONOMICS®

Weyerhaeuser | Barbara Ector
Consultant | Teacher

April 10, 2000
Date

▲ Junior Achievement®

© 1998 Junior Achievement Inc., M104
CERTIFICATE–Activity 10

CERTIFICATE
OF
Attendance
Cleveland City Schools

THIS CERTIFIES THAT

Victor Hill

HAS BEEN IN ATTENDANCE EVERY DAY FOR THE SCHOOL YEAR

_1997 - 1998_

_____   _Ann B. Culbreth_
Teacher   Principal

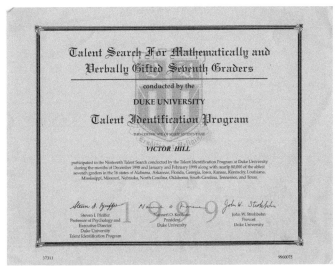

Talent Search For Mathematically and
Verbally Gifted Seventh Graders

conducted by the

DUKE UNIVERSITY

Talent Identification Program

THIS CERTIFICATE OF MERIT ATTESTS THAT

VICTOR HILL

participated in the Nineteenth Talent Search conducted by the Talent Identification Program at Duke University during the months of December 1998 and January and February 1999 along with nearly 80,000 of the ablest seventh graders in the 16 states of Alabama, Arkansas, Florida, Georgia, Iowa, Kansas, Kentucky, Louisiana, Mississippi, Missouri, Nebraska, North Carolina, Oklahoma, South Carolina, Tennessee, and Texas.

Steven I. Pfeiffer
Professor of Psychology and
Executive Director
Duke University
Talent Identification Program

Nannerl O. Keohane
President,
Duke University

John W. Strohbehn
Provost
Duke University

1999

37311   9960075

President's Education Awards Program

presented to

Victor Hill

in recognition of

Outstanding Academic Achievement

Dick Riley   1998   _Bill Clinton_

U.S. Secretary of Education   President of the United States

Ann B. Culbreth   _E. L. Ross_
Principal   School

NAME HILL   VICTOR   M

TEACHER	002	DAVIS	LEVEL	15
SCHOOL	0022	ERNEST L ROSS E	GRADE	5.7
SYSTEM	00061	CLEVELAND CITY	TEST DATE	4 97
SSN	414-63-5416		RUN DATE	5/17/97
ID	08801838			

Tennessee Comprehensive
Assessment Program

NORM REFERENCED

Copyright ©1990 by Tennessee Dept. of Education
All Rights Reserved. Printed in the USA.

SUBTESTS	SS	NCE	NS	NP	NP RANGE
READING VOCABULARY	793	92	9	98	93-99
READING COMPREHENSION	750	63	6	72	56-86
TOTAL READING	772	80	8	92	84-96
LANGUAGE MECHANICS	793	91	9	97	88-99
LANGUAGE EXPRESSION	745	57	6	63	48-78
TOTAL LANGUAGE	769	76	7	89	77-96
MATH COMPUTATION	*852	*99	*9	*99	94-99
MATH CONCEPTS & APPL.	782	80	8	93	82-97
TOTAL MATHEMATICS	807	99	9	99	93-99
TOTAL BATTERY	783	89	9	97	93-99
SPELLING	788	86	9	96	82-99
STUDY SKILLS	747	61	6	70	56-82
SCIENCE	777	75	7	88	80-94
SOCIAL STUDIES	783	77	8	90	83-95

NATIONAL PERCENTILE

1 2   5   10   20 30 40 50 60 70 80   90   95   98 99

1 2 3   4 5 6   7 8   9
BELOW AVERAGE STANINES   AVERAGE STANINES   ABOVE AVERAGE STANINES

LEGEND

SS	SCALE SCORE
NCE	NORMAL CURVE EQUIV.
NS	NATIONAL STANINE
NP	NATIONAL PERCENTILE
RANGE	LOW NP – HIGH NP
*	MAX/MIN SCORE
A	NO VALID ATTEMPT
N/A	NOT APPLICABLE

DOMAINS	SCORE	TENNESSEE CRITERION REFERENCED			LEGEND
		NON MASTERY	PARTIAL MASTERY	MASTERY	
LANGUAGE MECHANICS	M				
LANGUAGE USAGE	M				N NON MASTERY
SENTENCE/PARAGRAPH	M				(0-49 PERCENT
SPELLING/WORD IDENT.	M				CORRECT)
READING COMPREHENSION	M				P PARTIAL MASTERY
LITERARY SKILLS	M				(50-74 PERCENT
REFERENCE STUDY	M				CORRECT)
NUMERATION	M				M MASTERY
WHOLE NUMBER/INTEGER	M				(75-100 PERCENT
FRACTIONS	M				CORRECT)
DECIMALS	M				* NOT ALL ITEMS
GRAPHS, ETC.	M				ATTEMPTED
MEASUREMENT	M				A NO VALID ATTEMPT
GEOMETRY	M				
PROB. SOLV./APPLIC.	M				
PROBABILITY/STATISTICS	P				

INTERPRETATION OF SCORES

THIS STUDENT'S PERFORMANCE MAY BE COMPARED WITH THAT OF A NATIONAL SAMPLE OF 5TH GRADE STUDENTS BY REFERRING TO THE NATIONAL PERCENTILE SCORES FOR THE NORM REFERENCED PORTION OF THE TEST (UPPER PART OF THE PAGE). THE NATIONAL PERCENTILE INDICATES THE PERCENTAGE OF STUDENTS NATIONALLY THAT SCORED BELOW THIS STUDENT. THIS STUDENT SCORED AT PERCENTILE 92 IN TOTAL READING, WHICH FALLS IN THE ABOVE AVERAGE RANGE; PERCENTILE 89 IN TOTAL LANGUAGE, WHICH IS IN THE ABOVE AVERAGE RANGE; AND PERCENTILE 99 IN TOTAL MATHEMATICS, WHICH IS IN THE ABOVE AVERAGE RANGE. THE STUDENT'S TOTAL BATTERY SCORE IS BETTER THAN ABOUT 97 PERCENT OF THE NATIONAL SAMPLE, AND FALLS IN THE ABOVE AVERAGE RANGE. THE CRITERION REFERENCED PORTION OF THE TEST (LOWER

Certificate of Award
This Certifies That
Victor Hill
of
E. L. Ross Elementary School
has been awarded this certificate for
Sixth Grade Graduation
Date May 22, 1998

Shannon Cline
TEACHER

Ann B. Culbreth
PRINCIPAL

The National Junior Beta Club

This Certifies that

Victor Hill

of the

E. L. Ross Elementary School

Because of outstanding character and achievement
has been elected to membership

this 30th day of April 1998

Certificate of Achievement

International Marketing Task

Victor Hill
Name

E. L. Ross
School

has successfully completed

OUR WORLD

Shirley Underwood   Shannon Cline
Consultant   Teacher

3/11/99
Date

Junior Achievement

Sundaes For Scholars

Awarded To:

Jamie Hill

On: April 20, 2001

For Showing Great Fortitude, Improvement, and Exhibiting Qualities of Good Citizenship.

By: The Junior Auxiliary of Cleveland

Brownie Troop 132

1997 - 1998 Membership
Awards & Recognitions

Jamie Hill

D.A.R.E.

TO RESIST DRUGS AND VIOLENCE.

This is to certify that

Victor Hill

has successfully completed the
Junior High / Middle School
Drug Abuse Resistance Education program
at

Cleveland Middle School

D.A.R.E. Officer

March 25, 1999
Date

Music Award

Jamie Hill

has participated with distinction in the
*Cleveland City Schools
Elementary Chorus*

In recognition of your contributions

this award is presented
this 6th day of April 2000

signed *Chorus Director*

CERTIFICATE OF APPRECIATION

Presented to

Victor Hill

**for participating with distinction in the
Church of God, Inc., YOUTH MINISTERIES
Program.
June 29 - 30, 2001**

*Rhoda M. Lane-Darling, Chairperson
Eld. Gerald Jones, Asst. Chairperson
Mrs. Lavada E. Gray, President/H.Y.P.U., Sunday School and Usher Board
Bishop H. Dudley, General Overseer*

Certificate of Membership

National Honor Society

of

Secondary Schools

This Certifies that

Victor Hill

was selected a member

of the *Cleveland High School* Chapter
of the
National Honor Society of Secondary Schools.
Membership is based on
Scholarship, Leadership, Service, and Character.

Given at
this 29th

day of October, 2001

SECRETARY NHS NATIONAL COUNCIL
DIRECTOR, DEPARTMENT OF
STUDENT ACTIVITIES
NASSP

ADVISER

EXECUTIVE DIRECTOR
NATIONAL ASSOCIATION OR
SECONDARY SCHOOL PRINCIPALS

PRINCIPAL

Cleveland City Schools

Cleveland
City Schools
Pathway to Excellence

SPELLING BEE

Presented To

Jamie Hill

FOR OUTSTANDING PERFORMANCE IN SPELLING

GIVEN THIS 6th. DAY OF March , 2001 .

Mildred L. Maupin
SPELLING BEE COORDINATOR

DIRECTOR OF SCHOOLS

EXCELLENCE

Cleveland Middle School

We, the undersigned, hereby declare that

Jamie Hill

has completed all academic requirements to be listed on the
Honor Roll of Cleveland Middle School for each grading period
of the 2001–2002 school year

May 20, 2002

Ashley Smith, Principal   Jeff Elliott, Assistant Principal

Cleveland Middle School
AWARD

Jamie Hill

is awarded this certificate for outstanding achievement
during the 2002-2003 school year.

May 23, 2003

Teacher   Teacher   Teacher   Teacher

United States Achievement Academy

ESTABLISHED 1975

National Commemorative Certificate

To all who may read these letters, Greetings:

Hereby it is certified that the United States Achievement Academy has conferred on

Jamie Renee Hill

the honor of

National Award Winner

in recognition of the satisfactory fulfillment of the requirements pertaining to this honor.

George Stevens

Executive Director, Dr. George Stevens

Date

Good Character Counts

7 - Red Award

PERSEVERANCE

Presented To _____Jamie Hill_____

Cara Shumaker, ...   _May 23, 2002_
Teachers   Date

Achievement Certificate

This certifies that

_____Jamie Hill_____

has satisfactorily completed a course in

DRIVER EDUCATION

consisting of at least _30_ hours of classroom instruction, discussion, and student

activity and at least _6_ hours of road instruction while at the wheel of an automobile.

This instruction was received at _Cleveland H.S._

during the period from _____8/9/06_____ to _____12/18/06_____

_____
Authorized Instructor

DREAM KEEPER AWARD

In recognition of your striving for academic excellence,
this certificate of award is presented to

Jamie R. Hill

on this the 21st day of January, 2002 at Cleveland, Tennessee
on the occasion of the year 2002 community celebration
of the life and dream of Dr. Martin Luther King, Jr.
by the Ministers' Fellowship of Cleveland - Bradley County
and the 100 Black Men of Bradley County, Inc.
May God bless you,
may you continue to strive,
and may you always be judged by the content of your character.
The dream is in your hands.

_____
Rev. Aubrey Ector
President – Ministers' Fellowship

_____
Mr. Drew Robinson
President – 100 Black Men

Cleveland High School

Certificate of Recognition

Presented to *Victor Hill* for

Freshman Honor Group

May 12, 2001
Date

Principal

Cleveland High School

This is to certify that

Victor Hill

has participated in

Baseball

for the *2001* season

COACH

BLUE RAIDERS

TENNESSEE School Boards Association

certifies that

Victor Hill

REPRESENTING

Cleveland High School

of

Cleveland City

served with distinction as a delegate to the

Student Congress on Policies in Education

MARCH 8, 2002

Barbara Prescott
TSBA President

Board Chairman

Dan Tollett
Executive Director

Superintendent

Bands of America
presents this certificate of achievement to

Victor Hill
Cleveland H.S.
Congratulations on your participation in the

Bands of America
Regional Championship Presented by **YAMAHA**
East Tennessee State University, Johnson City, TN
September 28, 2002

YAMAHA

Cleveland High School
Certificate of Recognition

Presented to _____ Victor Hill _____ for

Hugh O'Brien Youth Leadership Program

May 17, 2002
Date

Principal

Ventures In Education, Inc.
is pleased to name

VICTOR HILL
as a

National Ventures Scholar

May 27, 2003

This certificate is awarded in recognition of your outstanding academic
achievement, dedication to excellence, and desire to pursue a career in
medicine and the allied health professions, math, science, engineering or technology.

Maxine E. Bleich
President, Ventures In Education, Inc.

VENTURES
SCHOLARS PROGRAM

Certificate of Invitation

NSLC

In recognition of academic excellence, extracurricular involvement,
and demonstrated leadership potential

Victor Hill

is hereby invited to participate in the
2003 National Student Leadership Conference.

This student meets the qualifications and requirements of the **NSLC**
Admissions Committee, and is invited to join other recognized student
leaders from across the United States and from more than 40 countries as
they come together to learn about, discuss and debate current issues in
Law, International Diplomacy, Congressional Policy, Medicine, Business, and Leadership.

On behalf of our Board of Directors and Honorary Board of Advisors
we extend our congratulations and hereunto affix our signatures.

Paul M. Lisnek, J.D. Ph.D.
Executive Director
Director of Academics

Mike Sims, Esq.
Executive Director
Director of Conferences

The Board of Directors of
Presidential Classroom
has conferred upon

Victor Hill

A Certificate of Achievement

in recognition of the successful completion of a Presidential Classroom Program

2004

John Barrasso, M.D., Chairman of the Board

The Honorable Jack Buechner, President & CEO

Maria Burgos
Instructor

Erin Monaco
Instructor

This is to certify that
VICTOR M. HILL
is represented in the
2002-2003
edition of

Who's Who Among American High School Students

Students, institutions and organizations recognized in this national
publication are to be commended for their high standards of excellence,
community leadership and positive performance.

Parke H. Davis, Publisher
Who's Who Among American High School Students®
HONORING TOMORROW'S LEADERS TODAY®

CERTIFICATE *of* ACHIEVEMENT

This is to certify that

VICTOR HILL

has been inducted into the

NATIONAL HONOR ROLL®

2002-2003

For Outstanding Academic and Community Achievement

2003

64th
Anniversary
AMERICAN LEGION
Boys' State

ATTENDANCE CERTIFICATE

This is to certify that

Victor M Hill   *of*   Crump

HAS ATTENDED AMERICAN LEGION BOYS' STATE

TENNESSEE TECHNOLOGICAL UNIVERSITY

Cookeville, Tennessee   May 25 - May 31, 2003

AND SERVED WITH HONOR IN THE OFFICE OF

Secretary of State

DIRECTOR   CHAIRMAN

CITY COUNSELOR   JUNIOR COUNSELOR

UNDER DIRECTION OF AMERICAN LEGION • DEPARTMENT OF TENNESSEE

DEPARTMENT ADJUTANT AMERICAN LEGION   DEPARTMENT COMMANDER AMERICAN LEGION

Certificate of Appreciation

Presented to

Victor Hill

Band Member of 2003 Tennessee
American Legion Boys' State

*In grateful appreciation and recognition of
distinguished service as a member of Tennessee's
2003 American Legion Boys' State Band.*

Presented in Cookeville, Tennessee, this 31st day of May, 2003.

Band Director   Department Chairman

Cleveland High School

Certificate of Recognition

Presented to   Victor Maurice Hill   for

Highest Distinction Senior Honor Group

May 15, 2004   *Chuck Rockholt*

Date   Principal

The National Society of High School Scholars

To Whom These Letters May Come

Greetings

This Certifies That

Victor Hill

in Recognition of Academic Achievement and Excellence, has been granted
Membership in The National Society of High School Scholars and is hereby
awarded all Rights, Honors, and Privileges thereunto appertaining.
This Membership is for Meritorious Scholastic Achievement
and the Pursuit of Excellence at

Cleveland High School

_____
Honorary Chair

_____
President

2003

Cleveland High School

Cleveland   Tennessee

This is to certify that

Victor Maurice Hill

has satisfied the requirements for graduation from High School
as prescribed by the Tennessee State Board of Education
and is therefore awarded this

Diploma

In Testimony Whereof and by the authority in us vested,
we have affixed our signatures this the twenty-first day of May, 2004.

_____
Frederick L. Denning
Superintendent of Schools

_____
Papa C. Seivers
Commissioner of Education

_____
Jacquelynn Wattenbarger
Chairman of the Board

_____
Chuck Rockholt
Principal

15

STATE OF TENNESSEE
By The Honorable
Dewayne Bunch
Member of the House of Representatives

CONGRATULATIONS
to
Victor Maurice Hill

upon your graduation from Cleveland High School. This noble achievement, the result of diligence, devotion, and dedication, is a major milestone in your life.

This is an expression of my confidence that you will continue to excel and achieve; that you will devote your life for the service of all mankind, which God has created; and that your life's calling shall bear the fruit of faith, hope and love.

In these endeavors, I offer you my best wishes and pray for God's blessing upon you. May you walk in the light and be the salt of this world.

Given under my hand, this
21ᵗ day of May, 2004

Dewayne Bunch
Dewayne Bunch
District 24

Bands of America
presents this certificate of achievement to

Jamie Hill
Cleveland H.S.

Congratulations on your participation in the

Bands of America
Regional Championship presented by YAMAHA®
Tropicana Field, St. Petersburg, FL
October 16, 2004

 YAMAHA
National Presenting Sponsor

L. Scott McCormick
President and CEO

THE NATIONAL SOCIETY OF THE

Daughters of the American Revolution

This certifies that

Victor Maurice Hill

having been selected as the DAR Good Citizen of

Cleveland High School

for the current year and having demonstrated the qualities of
Dependability, Service, Leadership and Patriotism,
is hereby awarded this
DAR Good Citizens Certificate

February 6, 2004
Date

National Chairman
DAR Good Citizens Committee

State Regent

President General
NSDAR

SIGNIFICANCE OF DAR GOOD CITIZEN'S PIN

Rim — 13 stars represent 13 original colonies.

Band of blue enamel identifies it with our Society.

Qualities of good character which we emphasize —
Dependability, Service, Leadership, Patriotism
are titles of four books in the center suggesting school days.

Circling these is the Laurel Wreath of Honor
behind them, the Torch of Understanding.

NATIONAL SOCIETY DAUGHTERS OF THE AMERICAN REVOLUTION
1776 D STREET NW, WASHINGTON, DC 20006–5303

REVISED JULY 2001

(0701–5000–PS)

Tennessee Gateway Assessment

Individual Profile Report

JAMIE HILL

Content: Science

Purpose
This report provides a comprehensive record of this student's performance. It is a source of information for instructional planning specific to the student and a point of reference for the teacher during a parent-teacher conference. It provides information regarding the student's performance on the Gateway Science examination which will be reflected in the student's cumulative record.

Birthdate: 02/23/88
Special Codes
ABCDEFGHIJKLMNOPQRST
41147887A.2.1. .....
Form: G

Test Date: 12/10/03

Teacher: SHARPE L C
School: CLEVELAND HIGH
System: CLEVELAND CITY
State: TENNESSEE GW FALL 03

CTB McGraw-Hill

Gateway Science Test Results

Your student has answered 39 items correctly on the Gateway Science examination. This score meets the Tennessee Science Gateway Requirement.

The Tennessee Gateway Science test data shown below describe your student's success in meeting the requirements of the content and skills assessed by this test.

This report shows that your student is proficient in: Cell Organelles and Biomolecules, Cell Processes, Interactions: Between Organisms and Behavior, Interactions: Population Dynamics and Energy Flow, Photosynthesis and Respiration, Genetics, Biotechnology/DNA, Diversity: Biomes and Classification, Diversity: Body Systems and Life Cycles.

The content and skills of Science represent one requirement for graduation from a Tennessee high school.

Performance on Reporting Categories

R.C. No.	Reporting Categories	Performance Level	RCPI
	Science		
01	Cell Organelles/Biomolecule	★	67
02	Cell Processes	★	59
03	Interactions: Org/Behavior	★	76
04	Interactions: Pop/Energy	★	76
05	Photosynthesis and Respir	★	62
06	Genetics	★	71
07	Biotechnology/DNA	★	76
08	Diversity: Biomes/Classif	★	91
09	Diversity: Body Sys/Life	★	54

Your student's performance on each one of the Science Reporting Categories is given on the left. The Performance Level for each Reporting Category is further designated as Below Proficient (designated by an open circle), Proficient (designated by a filled circle), or Advanced (designated by a filled star). The Reporting Categories Performance Index (RCPI) is an estimate of the number of items your student would be expected to answer correctly if there had been 100 such items for that category. For example, a RCPI score of 67 for Cell Organelles and Biomolecules indicates that your student would correctly answer 67 out of 100 questions in that category. The bands to the right and left of the diamond (Confidence Band) represents the range where the student would most likely score in a similar test experience.

◇ : Your Reporting Category Performance Index | Represents the Minimum Reporting Category Performance Index for a Proficient Student   ─── : Confidence Band

Performance Level Indicators
★ Advanced
● Proficient
○ Below Proficient

CTB/ID: 04044M022207003-04-00905-000344

Tennessee Gateway Assessment

Individual Profile Report

JAMIE HILL

Content: Mathematics

Purpose
This report provides a comprehensive record of this student's performance. It is a source of information for instructional planning specific to the student and a parent-teacher conference. It provides information regarding the student's performance on the Gateway Mathematics examination which will be reflected in the student's cumulative record.

Birthdate: 02/23/88
Special Codes
ABCDEFGHIJKLMNOPQRST
41147887A.1.1. .....
Form: G

Test Date: 12/09/03

Teacher: ADCOCK J A
School: CLEVELAND HIGH
System: CLEVELAND CITY
State: TENNESSEE GW FALL 03

CTB McGraw-Hill

Gateway Mathematics Test Results

Your student has answered 47 items correctly on the Gateway Mathematics examination. This score meets the Tennessee Mathematics Gateway Requirement.

The Tennessee Gateway Mathematics test data shown below describe your student's success in meeting the requirements of the content and skills assessed by this test.

This report shows that your student is proficient in: Number Sense/Theory, Algebraic Expressions, Equations and Inequalities, Real World Problems, Graphs and Graphing, Spatial Sense and Geometric Concepts.

The content and skills of Mathematics represent one requirement for graduation from a Tennessee high school.

Performance on Reporting Categories

R.C. No.	Reporting Categories	Performance Level	RCPI
	Mathematics		
01	Number Sense/Theory	★	89
02	Algebraic Expressions	★	87
03	Equations and Inequalities	★	85
04	Real World Problems	★	85
05	Graphs and Graphing	★	85
06	Spatial/Geometric Concepts	★	82

Your student's performance on each one of the Mathematics Reporting Categories is given on the left. The Performance Level for each Reporting Category is further designated as Below Proficient (designated by an open circle), Proficient (designated by a filled circle), or Advanced (designated by a filled star). The Reporting Categories Performance Index (RCPI) is an estimate of the number of items your student would be expected to answer correctly if there had been 100 such items for that category. For example, a RCPI score of 89 for Number Sense/Theory indicates that your student would correctly answer 89 out of 100 questions in that category. The bands to the right and left of the diamond (Confidence Band) represents the range where the student would most likely score in a similar test experience.

◇ : Your Reporting Category Performance Index | Represents the Minimum Reporting Category Performance Index for a Proficient Student   ─── : Confidence Band

Performance Level Indicators
★ Advanced
● Proficient
○ Below Proficient

CTB/ID: 04044M022207001-04-00811-000268

From the desk of
Jefferey J. Fix

Who's Who ID #: 37261654-4

Jamie R. Hill and Family
2067 Woodvale St. NW
Cleveland TN 37311-3506

Response Requested By
May 26, 2006

Dear Jamie:

Your biography has been accepted for publication in *Who's Who Among American High School Students*®, 2005-2006. Since only 5% of the students from our nation's 24,000 high schools are honored in *Who's Who* each year, we commend you for your achievements. You may want to celebrate this honor with your family.

Please remember, there are no financial responsibilities attached to this award. Because many students want a copy of the book and other award insignia as a memento of this honor, a catalog is enclosed for your consideration.

You are now automatically eligible to compete for one of 61 scholarships awarded each year ranging from $1,000 to $6,000. Over $4,000,000 has been awarded through this program to date. Your application is enclosed.

You may now also use *The College Referral Service*® (CRS), a reference service for college-bound *Who's Who* students exclusively. With the CRS, you can designate which colleges you wish us to notify of your acceptance into *Who's Who*. Recent surveys indicate that nearly 90% of responding college admissions directors use the *Who's Who* when considering students for admissions. Each year over 100,000 referrals are made for *Who's Who* students. The CRS catalog and application are enclosed.

The attached form also provides an opportunity for you to nominate a teacher whom you wish to honor in *Who's Who Among America's Teachers*®. When evaluating the teachers who "made a difference" in your life, please remember to consider teachers from your earliest years who may have influenced your current success.

With every good wish for the future,

Jefferey J. Fix
Jefferey J. Fix
Vice President of Student Programs

Enclosures: Four (4)

P.S. You may place your order on our secure web site, www.whoswho-highschool.com using your *Who's Who* ID number.

DETACH HERE

WHO'S WHO AMONG AMERICAN HIGH SCHOOL STUDENTS
7211 Circle S Road • Austin, TX 78745 • (877) 843-9946 • www.whoswho-highschool.com

18

NSLC

Leadership Excellence
Since 1989

Certificate of Invitation

In recognition of academic excellence and demonstrated leadership potential,

Jamie Hill

is hereby invited to represent the city of Cleveland at the
2006 National Student Leadership Conference Tennessee Leadership Workshop.

We congratulate you and look forward to welcoming you and other recognized student leaders from across the state of Tennessee
to learn about, discuss and experience the skills of effective leaders.

**On behalf of our Board of Directors and Honorary Board of Advisors we extend our
congratulations and hereunto affix our signatures**

Paul M. Lisnek, J.D., Ph.D.
Executive Director
Director of Academics

Mike Sims, J.D.
Executive Director
Director of Conferences

National Student Leadership Conference   111 West Jackson Blvd., 7th Floor   Chicago, IL 60604   800-977-6752   Fax 312-765-0081   www.nslcstates.org

---

Certificate of Invitation

*In recognition of academic excellence,
extracurricular involvement and
leadership potential*

*The Board of Directors
and
Honorary Board of Advisors
Invite*

Jamie R. Hill

to attend the

*2006
Congressional Student Leadership Conference
sponsored by
LeadAmerica*

19

Distinguished Alumni
National Youth Leadership Forum

Cleveland High School

Miss Jamie Hill
Medicine 2006 Nominee

Miss Rebecca Davis Medicine 2004	Mr. Andrew Disbrow Medicine 2004
Miss Christina Schmitt Medicine 2004	Miss Whitney Phillips Medicine 2003
Miss Kate Loney Medicine 2003	Miss Nelum Porte Medicine 2001
Miss Amy McIntosh Medicine 2000	Miss Memorie Shaw Medicine 1998
Mr. Philip Schmitt Technology 2005	

Dream Keeper Award

In recognition of your striving for academic excellence,
this certificate of award is presented to

Jamie R. Hill

on this the 15th day of January, 2007 at Cleveland, Tennessee
on the occasion of the year 2007 community celebration
of the life and dream of Dr. Martin Luther King, Jr.
by the Bradley County NAACP, Ministers' Fellowship of Cleveland - Bradley County,
and the 100 Black Men of Bradley County, Inc.
May God bless you,
may you continue to strive,
and may you always be judged by the content of your character.
The dream is in your hands.

Lawrence Armstrong
Bradley County NAACP, President

Rev. Aubrey Ector
Ministers' Fellowship, President

Mr. Charles Swafford, IV
100 Black Men, President

The National Society of High School Scholars

To whom these letters may come

Greetings

This certifies that

JAMIE R. HILL

in recognition of academic achievement and excellence, has been granted membership in The National Society of High School Scholars and is hereby awarded all rights, honors, and privileges thereunto appertaining. This membership is for meritorious scholastic achievement and the pursuit of excellence at

CLEVELAND HIGH SCHOOL

Founder & Chairman, NSHSS
Nobel Prize Family

President
The National Society of High School Scholars

2006

Certificate of Recognition

CLEVELAND · BRADLEY
CHAMBER OF COMMERCE

Cleveland City Schools
Pathway to Excellence

presented to

Jamie Hill

for accepting challenges, setting high goals and fulfilling the requirements to graduate as a

2007 Tennessee Scholar

Brenda Lawson
Chairman of the Board
Cleveland/ Bradley Chamber of Commerce

Tennessee Scholars Coordinator
Cleveland/ Bradley Chamber of Commerce

TENNESSEE SCHOLARS
WORLD-CLASS STUDENTS

Director
Cleveland City Schools

Principal
Cleveland High School

STATE OF TENNESSEE
By the Honorable

Senator Dewayne Bunch ∞ Representative Kevin Brooks

Members of the 105th Tennessee General Assembly
offer their
CONGRATULATIONS
To

Jamie Renee Hill

upon your graduation from *Cleveland High School*. This noble achievement, the result of diligence, devotion, and dedication, is a major milestone in your life.

This is an expression of our confidence that you will continue to excel and achieve; that you will devote your life to God's calling; and that your life's endeavors will always strive to be in the light and that you shall be the salt of this earth.

In these endeavors, we offer you our *BEST WISHES.*
May God Bless and Keep You.

Given under our hands, this
17th day of May, 2007

Senator Dewayne Bunch
9th District

Representative Kevin Brooks
24th District

IN HONOR OF
OUTSTANDING ACADEMIC ACHIEVEMENT
People to People Ambassador Programs

congratulates

Jamie Hill

on graduating from the 2006 Leadership Summit and accepting the challenge to promote understanding and citizenship and to be a leader in the community.

Mary Jean Eisenhower,
President and CEO of People to People International

Jeffrey D. Thomas,
CEO of People to People Ambassador Programs

Cleveland High School

Cleveland   Tennessee

This is to certify that

Jamie Renée Hill

has satisfied the requirements for graduation from High School as prescribed by the Tennessee State Board of Education and is therefore awarded this

Diploma

In Testimony Whereof and by the authority in us vested, we have affixed our signatures this the seventeenth day of May, 2007.

Superintendent of Schools

Chairman of the Board

Commissioner of Education

Principal

Printed in the United States
By Bookmasters